The Sexual Wilderness

The Wilderness Romance Part 2

Freshwater

Freshwater Press, USA

All Scripture references taken from the KJV of the Holy Bible, unless otherwise indicated.

freshwaterpress9@gmail.com

The Sexual Wilderness: *The Wilderness Romance, Part 2*

https://marlenemilestheauthor.com/

Follow the Author on Instagram and Twitter.

Paperback Version

ISBN# 978-1-893555-93-8

Freshwater Press

United States of America

Contents

Foreword

This book is about the Sexual Wildernesses where anyone can get lost. It is a dangerous place, easy to fall into and hard to get out of. We will discuss how people get there and how to get out. The purpose of The Sexual Wilderness it to keep you and others from getting into Wilderness relationships and even Wilderness Marriages.

God always provides a way of escape, even from the Wilderness.

Part 2
The Sexual Wilderness

Because of choices made and
compromises taken,
It as though the Wilderness hunts you down.

The Wilderness is the bad choice,
or the compromise prison.
The Wilderness Romance is not about God's ideal,
because fortunately, most of us don't live there.

It's about what to do when you've
done the human thing,
but realized subsequently,
that there is a better way.

What Has God Made?

If you are one who doesn't have a spouse, do you feel that it's hopeless? Do you worry that God won't unite you in marital and holy bliss? These thoughts may lead to worry or anxiety and can lead to making hasty, Wilderness decisions. Instead, walk circumspectly and know who you are. Don't seek marriage for the sake of marriage. Marriage, as man knows it is **not** *The Promise*. If it were, for the cost a marriage license you could get you all you want in life, but it doesn't. So don't look for a man for the sake of a man. A man is not The Promise.

Don't get pregnant for the sake of having a child. That is not God's way; that is not The Promise. Unless you are the ONE and God has told you that you will have a child of Promise!

O Lord, our Lord, how excellent is thy name in all the Earth. who hast set thy glory above the heavens? What is man, that thou art mindful of him and the son of man, that Thou visitest him. Thou hast made him a little lower than Elohim. And has crowned him with glory and honor. O Lord, our Lord, how excellent is thy name in all the earth (Psalm 8).

You've worked so hard to become someone who would be an asset and desirable to a desirable man. Yeah, but where is he? *You visit me, Lord* why won't anyone else? Where's my man? Where's my Adam, you may be asking? Maybe you made one or two major mistakes in life. Who hasn't? You've done everything possible to correct those mistakes. Yet where is he? We see friends and family members in loving relationships, where is yours? You've worked seemingly through impossible odds to make yourself presentable and attractive. Not just physically, but also intellectually and emotionally.

You have admitted and worked at your own known spiritual problems. You don't harbor resentment and hatred anymore. You've sought soul restoration. You have unloaded all the negative baggage that women are accused of carrying. Where is he? Why does it seem as though no man wants you?

Can it be that God has called you to be single? How can you honorably be fruitful and multiply if you're single? Why is it so cold or lonely at night? If you're called to be single, the Comforter would surely be doing His job, and I don't mean the down comforter on your bed, either. Why would God put, or allow desire for mate to be in you if you are *called* to be single? You probably aren't called to be single, just as Adam, our first and natural example wasn't. If God says so, He has someone for you and not just anyone, but a *certain someone*. That God is offering you a *certain someone* doesn't give you permission to be picky in the flesh. Yes. You can be picky about the spirit that you'll be united with, but flesh should not take the lead in this decision or any other of your important life decisions.

Mismatched

You may feel that you are mismatched right now, but you *may* be married to the right person. For example, I know a church pastor who does not know that his wife of 18 years, is an **atheist**. She probably has a box to put God in, and He won't fit, so she can't fathom God. Who can? God is deep. Is this man married to the right woman? I don't know. Maybe she does not believe in God, but she may be the right person for him. She may have to *become* the right person for him. Yes, God does exist, and He is real. God can still save the unsaved and when an unsaved mate receives salvation more than just the angels rejoice. Perhaps, like Hosea and Gomer, this particular pastor *should* be married to this atheist. Perhaps there's a lesson to them both. Perhaps it's the thrust of their ministry together--, once the pastor realizes or discerns it, and his wife gets saved. God knows.

If you've been married to someone who just got saved after 20 years, for example, that may mean that you married them in the wrong season. It doesn't mean you married the wrong person, but you married them at the wrong time. Through the years, there are many *right now's* that people have acted on, but then later on found out it was the wrong person. But you can marry the *right* person in the **wrong now**. Don't be in such a hurry; *right now* can cause a quick fall into the Wilderness.

Perhaps the mate God had intended you to be married to is married to one of those people who believes that all men are the same, or all women are the same. They may be married to a wonderful, unique individual that they may find odd or strange. What they perceive as *strange* could perfectly be suited for another of God's chosen, a chosen such as you. But don't covet.

God took an Eve out of every Adam, I believe that the rib needs to be reunited with its body, and the body with its rib. There's one Adam that matches his Eve, and vice versa. Anything different may cause a foreign body reaction, or rejection. That's what men are doing when they search for the right woman; they're looking for their rib. And who better to know? It came from them.

However, most men for some reason believe that they had a 36-24-36 rib from which God made their Eve. (There is deliverance for this.) Look at the mirror, man, seriously what do you think *your rib* would make? Look at your baby pictures, your sisters, and brothers. Do you have any natural children? Look at them. Those are the people of your your gene pool; your rib will make something similar.

Dating

When you are mismatched in your dating life, what do you do? You break it off. Dating can be fun and simple if you remember these pointers.

- o Dating is for the purpose of seeing who you may want to marry, says Kimberly Trice.
- o Dating is not for sex.
- o Dating is not for dining out or getting gifts.

- Dating is not to find a man who looks OK and *remake* him.
- Dating is not to find a man that has financial security, and then convert him into who you want him to be.
- Dating is not pre-marriage, pretending to be married or *playing house*. Dating is not a dry run or test to see if you like marriage; they're completely different things.

Dating cannot be marriage because there is no anointing to be or stay married until God joins two together. In dating the man and the woman both know there are no permanent strings; they can leave anytime they choose.

- Pretending to be married is very dangerous, whether you're married or not. That's like pretending to be saved, which is pretending to be married to, and in covenant with God.

Married

Every marriage was not made in Heaven and ordained of God. Every marriage wasn't put together by God. Whether you were married on a ship, in City Hall, in a church, in a cathedral, or on a beach has no bearing on whether *God* joined the two of you together. Ever see the most beautiful man with the most horrible woman and wonder to yourself, *How did **that** happen?* Or the converse. Every marriage isn't put together by God.

There's a certain type of woman, for instance, who is usually gorgeous, who could marry the most dear, considerate, and wonderful man treat, him horribly and make his life hell. Is she the problem, or is he? They both are. If he chose her for physical reasons only, then that's his problem.

Did God put them together? I don't know. Does God care what we do in the physical, or is our God only spiritual? Spiritually, can two who are completely different even be *yoked?* Should they be? The Bible says that two cannot walk together except they be agreed (Amos 3:3). A Wilderness Man can make it clear to you that he likes your body, and you can agree that you think you're brick house and it's about time somebody noticed. But, that kind of agreement won't get you two walking anywhere together. *Walking* is not what he has in mind. Being *yoked* for work, especially ministry, is not what he has in mind either. So, ladies, watch what you agree to.

Women Whom Men Loved

Abraham sent his servant to get a wife for his son, Isaac.

A woman such as Rebecca was intreated as a precious prize of honor and virtue. Jacob, Isaac's son vies for the hand of Rachel for 7 years, ends up with Leah at first, but works seven more years for Rachel. How many men do you know or have ever heard of who would--?

- o Work for the woman they love.
- o Work 14 years for the woman they love?

That's the kind of man God has for you.

Most of the work a man has to do and has to allow to be done is on *himself.* Just as the work you have to do, and have to have done is on *you*. When the man works to be what God has called him to be, then he's preparing and getting ready to receive an Eve, a Rebecca, or a Rachel, a highly prized, virtuous woman.

Man has to work to prepare a place, a home for you. He needs to have a satisfying and fulfilling career, means to take care of you. Let him do that first, then let him *send for* you. Get out of his way while he's working. Get out of God's way while that man is being worked on.

A man who is developed physically may only consider the physical. A man who's developed intellectually will stress intellect in a relationship. A man who's developed spiritually will seek a *spiritually* compatible mate. The man who's fully developed will seek a fully developed spouse. Balance in development is the key. If you've only developed *part* of yourself, that may be why you're attracting the man who rates himself high in that area or sees that you rate high in that area, while the rest may go lacking.

Developing a prissiness, which is, in my opinion, over-developed femininity wasn't even attractive in Bible times.

The tender and delicate woman among. You, which would not adventure to set the sole of her foot upon the ground for delicateness and tenderness, eye shall be evil toward the husband of her bosom , and toward her son, and toward her daughter. (Deuteronomy 28:56)

A Godly man is not overly interested in this type of woman. A worldly man may like it, but God's man wants a comely daughter of Zion., (Jeremiah 6:2), a virtuous woman, (Proverbs 31). A fully developed, real man, the kind who think you want, is looking for a fully developed real woman, and a woman in relationship with God. Affectations such as prissiness, might be a fantasy, but in the long term, the day-to-day, they are not that attractive to men. Women, all the flowing hair weaves, false nails, and eyelashes --face it, they are for other women. Most men don't notice if your hair is long or short, purple or red. Haven't you noticed that most of your compliments from your dress to your shoes to your hairstyle comes from *other women*? Look good, but don't waste so much money and time on it. Instead, be sure to develop yourself *spiritually*, and be physically healthy. Develop your soul by growing emotionally and intellectually, and financially. Don't spend all day in the hair salon and at the mall adorning your flesh.

If you have allowed God to make you, then you are a precious commodity. You are in demand, yet you must use discernment when seeking a Kingdom marriage. Somebody really wants you; you are just right to and for somebody. Your cooking style, body type, sense of humor, or lack of, the way you can sing or can't is just right for the somebody that God has for you. Be assured, if you are Promised Land person, God will not yoke you with a Wilderness Man.

What has God made that no one wants? Nothing.

Everything that God has made is good. That's why the world wants it. Marriage, for instance, is God's institution. Yet the world tries to take it for theirs. You see blatant sinners in white dresses feigning purity. But God cannot be mocked (Galatians 6:7). The glorious wedding pictures of the bride in white, and the groom in tails, with all the trimmings, with the couple's six out of wedlock children *in* the ceremony. You know the six they've had since they've been living together for the past ten years. Parents, your child's innocence is not imputed to you, even in your wedding pictures that you cannot wait to post online.

But it's the world; they do as they like.

Folks, your *guilt* may be imputed to your children unless Jesus is in the picture. When choosing temptation or opportunities to live right, be mindful of what you're doing to your children, even *before* you conceive them.

Marriage must have a head. **If the individuals aren't saved, then the devil is still the head of their lives**. Whomever is the head of their lives is head of their marriage. Pretending to be married? Who are you kidding? Releasing doves, God's symbol of peace, the symbol of the Holy Spirit, making covenant on the ring finger as in Old Testament custom? Borrowing spiritual things and spiritual symbols but not living God's way will not keep anyone married any more than wearing crosses and crucifixes will get anyone to Heaven. Legally, the couple mentioned here is married with the state and federal government as their head, on paper. That means they can do anything the government approves and still be married legally, but not necessarily *spiritually* married. That's why divorce is no big thing to the person who is only <u>legally</u> married. It's just a matter of paperwork.

What has God made? If God made you, He has also made someone *for* you. Rest in that, walk-in that, live in that. Women of God be all you can be so you can have all that you're supposed to have.

The Man Safari

Ladies, the first thing you need to know about searching for a man is **don't search for a man.** Why? When you look for things, you find things. Sometimes you find things you don't want to find. At other times you may find things that *look like* things you want to find. No one who was not *looking* for an oasis has ever found a mirage of an oasis. Your desire plays an important part in what you see, hear, and find. If you're out looking for a man in the desert of life where you think there are no men, or no good men, you may find the *mirage* of a man. You might marry that man, and then OMG! You'll be so sorry to find out he was *acting* all along and is not even real! A *mirage* of a man!

The Bible says seek first the Kingdom, **not** *seek first the man*. So don't set out on a manhunt; seek God, then **let the man find you**.

But if you're out in the wild, on a ***Man Safari***, even if you're just looking, you might find you are being noticed, looked at, searched out. Pay attention; keep your eyes open and *look back*. Look to see *who's* looking at you. What you see is what you get. And sometimes what you *don't* see is what you get. Many times, there are hidden things that must be uncovered, revealed, and discussed before entering into a serious long-term, permanent relationship. People do not normally puts their flaws, shortcomings, and issues on display, so do your looking, now. Look deep, whenever possible.

Man Safari Rules

The **First Rule** of the **Man Safari**: Don't go hunting.

Second Rule: Dress appropriately, look nice--not vulgar; you don't have to put it *all* out there, Do not create a frenzy. If you draw *everything*, most often it will be all the *wrong everything*. The good ones don't follow the *thirsty* crowd. The good ones are smart, confident, and do not give in to peer pressure. Appropriate shoes are needed in case you have to suddenly get away. Go with a *covering* for your head, the sun blazes in the desert.

The Man Safari is very interesting because even while you're in a place of "hunting", your job is to *not* look for a man. Be bold, be Scriptural. Don't look; but be prepared always as you allow *him* to do his job and look for **you**. Be available for him to *find* you. Look good and don't try to play hard to get; that's so high school.

Consider the picture taking safari. You're out there. The wild animals are all around you, but you're not shooting, trapping, or taking any of these animals home; you're taking *pictures*. Just pictures. True, you are looking at what could be looking at you but don't be too obvious.

Third Rule: Don't be too aggressive, the good ones don't like a lot of aggression; they find it distasteful. Over confidence or aggression could either scare them away or cause one of them to charge after you. Find the right balance between confidence and aloofness.

Fourth Rule: Don't fear; they can sense fear and may attack; they may try to take advantage of you if they sense fear.

Fifth Rule: Behave as if you're *not* on a **Man Safari**.

Sixth Rule: Remember other people, and especially men, are on Safari too. Be courteous to your fellow safarists – male and female. Biblically, culturally, traditionally, men have always had *permission* to do more than just take pictures of the gazelle or the lioness that they may want to take home. Mostly because they *men* gave *men* permission to do all that **extra** stuff.

Give yourself permission to be out there, *looking*.

Seventh Rule: Go ahead, take your pictures, Girl. Focus. God has revealed many things to me through real and virtual cameras. And He can do the same for you.

o Stop looking in bad places for good men. Don't look in clubs, bars, casinos, and lounges, unless that's the type you're looking for.

Of course, if that's where you hang out, all will presume that's the kind of man you want. Wherever you spend your time, it stands to reason that the person with similar interests will be in that place.

o Stop looking _at_ the wrong men.
o Married men are off limits in case your momma never told you.

Here's a practical rule of thumb. If you like the married man's package, that is, his clothes, car, house, and money, **and he's married**, mentally DIVIDE that package in half _or less_. Now, do you still like what you see? That's what you'll get when he's divorced-- if you get him at all. If he's playing around with on *her*, he'll play around on you.

Oh, and you'll get lots of court dates, lawyers, stress and he will be spending his money on child support and visitation weekends. Baby mamma's and ex-wives NEVER go away. Add that to the list of stuff you'll get if you break up a marriage.

A woman doesn't *cause* a male to fool around, it's something that's in him that *he* chooses to do. His current wife or Ex is not the problem, no matter what he tells you. *Chronic dissatisfaction is* **Wilderness** *and* there's deliverance for that.

Wilderness Men

If you're on a safari, chances are that most of the men out there *are* **Wilderness Men**. Take the mental, virtual picture but leave him there. Even if you catch what looks like a trophy bass, throw it back, if it's from the Lake of the Wilderness.

But if you find a man who is just traveling *through* the Wilderness, on the way to somewhere real, or traveling through with his Wilderness Bruh's, that's another whole story. That would be a good catch, *once he catches you.* Take the picture, take it home, make sure it's developed properly; take the filters off it—look past the haze and the retouches. Who is this man, really?

Now, show the picture, if not the entire man, to your daddy. That's both your natural father and your heavenly Father and tell them, "*This is so, and so.*" Then let them tell you if this is a **Wilderness Man** or not before you commence to dating.

If you don't have a natural father, show the man to the man who is your covering, or whomever has authority over you--, Uncle, Deacon, Elder, Pastor--, somebody. And always ask God, *"I've met this guy. Is this a divine connection, or an evil connection? Do I continue with him?"* Ask that early in the connection.

- o Males who have not become **men** are off limits. That means teenagers, overgrown boys, and the immature who have not left

Mommy or who have not defined their manhood, and masculinity as God defines it are off limits.

o Playa's and OG's are off limits. If he tells you one lie, how many other lies do you think he has? No one has just ONE lie.

o You're not dating his **potential**, so no Men-by-Faith. You wouldn't eat a bowl of un-popped popcorn, would you? Wait for him to go through his *process.*

o Males whose lives are discombobulated are off limits. Let a man stabilize and settle down on his own. If not, he may always resent you for "making" him do something he didn't think he was *ready* for.

You don't know what a fellow has gone through and what he has yet to go through to regroup. If you see a fellow who hasn't gone through anything but is still discombobulated quick, get away from him. Run!

Further, a steady eye-diet of *looking* at those types will keep you thinking that that's all there is, or that there are not any decent men around. But that's not all there is. There **are** many decent men available.

- o You cannot change the gender preference of a man. They are also off limits. Don't fall prey to the confused or downlow ones but pray for them.
- o Stop looking at unsaved men, they are also off limits; they are not ready. The Bible says you should not be unequally yoked.

A yoke in agrarian culture was for work. Do not be unequally united with someone *outside* of the work that God has sent you here to do. An unsaved man gives no thought and has no intention of doing *spiritual work.* You cannot save a man, only God does that, but you can pray and witness to him with the right motives. Your own personal use is not a right motive, no matter how good looking he is.

If you've gotten saved since you married your husband, Glory! But that is not necessarily grounds to divorce *him.* It only proves that you married him *out of season.* If both of you were unsaved, you were both out of season. I'm not saying unsaved folk can't get married, the Bible says that one can sanctify their unsaved spouse. Seek God and counseling on this matter.

Rule Eight: Don't feed them. He is to "audition" for you, not you for him. Let him take you out, do not take him home and feed him as if you two are married already. Go someplace nice, not a burger joint or a drive thru. I mean it.

Rule Nine of the Safari is go on a Saved Safari, if at all possible, make it a Spirit-filled Safari. For the very enlightened, make your safari a Saved-, Spirit-filled-, Purpose-led-, Destiny-Driven- Safari. You'll be much happier once you allow yourself to be *caught* by such a human animal. The more specific you are, especially in prayer life, the better results you have. You can be as picky as you want spiritually, but woman of God, don't waste time on being picky over flesh issues. Why? Because flesh is subject to change from one day to the next.

- o Stop looking at any kind who is not the right kind of man.

But when on Safari and if he's looking at you, when you look in his direction, look at **all of him**. Do you still have your camera? Ready? Aim, focus. Don't forget to focus.

Remember when you were in high school you went out with a guy because he was cute? Cute does not a husband make. Move past the face. What do you really see? Focus. When do you look, don't limit your looking to the physical or the financial. How is he emotionally, mentally, intellectually, and most importantly, spiritually.

How do the two of you match up socially? He may be too advanced for you, or vice versa in any category. Be realistic.

What track is he on for advancement? Any? Or is he complacent where he is? Is he through growing? Is he ready to retire from life?

What is his purpose in life? What is yours? Does he have the time to accomplish his Purpose; is he realistic? Does he know his purpose? Do yours and his complement one another?

How does he relate to family, friends, people in general? If no flags go up, he might be a good person to date and to get to know better.

Rule Ten of the **Man Safari** is: **Be yourself**.

Man Safari Warnings

Also, to aid you in your non-searching **Man Safari** are the following **warnings**. Proceed with your eyes wide open and especially note men who are:

- o **Only children**.
- o **Only sons**.
- o **Oldest sons**.
- o **Favored sons**.
- o **Sons with no fathers**, especially those who have been the man and breadwinner of the family.
- o **Unsaved men. Men with suspicious *religions*. Men from families of suspicious**

religions or unusual spiritual practices. Don't bring trouble on yourself.

- o **Sons of needy** hurt, irrational, and unsaved **mothers**.
- o **Sons with controlling mothers.**
- o Beautiful mothers make beautiful sons but beware of **vain mothers**.
- o **Jealous mothers.**
- o Also watch out, but to a lesser degree for **the jealous sister**. I've been told that in some cultures the jealous sister is worse than a jealous mother.
- o In rare cases, the **jealous brother**. Remember how Aaron and Miriam treated Moses after he married the Ethiopian woman? (Numbers 12.)

These warnings are by no means engraved in stone. These are just notes on what I've seen and been told over the years. You might be blessed enough to meet a quality man with a loving, normal family. I certainly hope so.

For best results you may use these **Man Safari Rules** or customize your safari by adding your own God-given rules and instructions.

Ladies: Don't fall into Desperation.
Desperation has men and facsimiles of men
who are just *dying* to meet you.

No Labels

Beware of the man, who says, *"I don't do labels."*
Do No Harm

In interpersonal relationships, I warn you: Do no harm. Do no harm to others. Doctor. Captain. Maestro, Astronaut, Race Car Driver, Superhero – whatever self-proclaimed title you are wielding to impress the other gender, the object of your desires. Do no harm to them. Do no harm to anyone you want to be in an interpersonal relationship with, or to anyone that you are pursuing in a romantic way. Do no harm to her physically, but definitely do no harm to her soul and/or spirit.

(I am using masculine pronouns to describe the aggressor in this chapter, but the genders are as they are in your life.)

In the natural, a man wants to sow seed. He believes it is his right to sow seed, but to sow it where and when? Herein lies the problem, and the problem is usually **lies**. Where is all this seed supposed to be going?

One of the most dangerous things on Earth is a spiritually unprotected person who either *thinks* he's protected, *pretends* he's protected, or doesn't have sense enough to know that he needs ***spiritual protection.***

What women most often want/expect from a relationship: in no particular order.

- o Companionship- A rue friend who accept you as you are and still invites you to grow.
- o To be oneself.
- o Physicality, possibly. Probably.
- o Fun, definitely.
- o Physical Protection, usually.
- o Emotional Stability and security.

o Financial Stability.

o Respect and Honor – to be celebrated, honored, treated well.

o Position. A woman needs clarity of her position, (man, don't you?).

Many men say they don't want to *put a label on* the relationship. Yeah, do that in your freezer or your pantry, don't label anything and see how long things last. See how much food, time, money you waste if you don't know what anything is, or how long it's been in the back corner of the pantry or deeply frozen in the deep freeze.

You cannot govern anything unless you name it says Prophet Kevin Leal. In Genesis God had Adam to name everything. Things and people don't need a name if you're not going to go back for them, not planning to make use of them again, or if you're never planning to call them again. You won't write their name and number or a scrap piece of paper, take their business card, or save them in your phone if you're never going to talk to them again, if they have no purpose in your life, or your future, they don't need a name.

If you are planning to see it, or them again, talk to them again, they need a Name. Period. You need to know what to call them.

I don't do labels is a commonly heard excuse in the Wilderness dating experience, even from an organized person who organizes things and uses labels.

God labeled us *man--*, mankind and called us Adam. We were both named Adam, male and female; later Adam named everything and gave the woman the name, Eve. Whatever Adam called a thing that was its name. Even your dog has a name, so when you call it, he/she trots over to you.

God created us a little lower than the angels and set us in dominion, with authority. **Now, if GOD told us not to worry about a label or a name, a position, don't worry about a relationship, just *go with the flow* and that He wasn't sure of what our relationship would be just yet, that would be a serious problem**. And that's how we know that this kind of talk is not God. This is devil talk, straight out of hell. This random talk where nothing is organized, labeled, called anything, or called what it's supposed to be is random, refried confusion.

If God doesn't treat us like that, then no one else <u>ever</u> should either, if we are God's children.

I challenge you that this man who doesn't like Labels:

- o Has a designer horse on his shirt pocket.
- o A peace sign, or a pony or some other swish on the front of his car or truck.
- o He has a well-chosen avatar on his social media page.
- o He's the man with a circle, a crown, or certain words over or under the 12 on his designer watch.
- o There's a crest with swords through it on his fragrance bottle.
- o He is the man who only uses name brand foods from the best name brand market.
- o He only dines here, only banks there, only buys gas at certain stations.
- o He's a man with a logo on his own business card as he promotes **himself** and **his** business ***Brand***.

So you see, Sir, ***all you do is labels.***

Woman of God, stay out of the dating Wilderness with such a talker. **Run! He wants to rope you into the Sexual Wilderness. He doesn't want** *relationship* **with you; he wants** <u>transactions</u> **that cost him nothing.**

Generic

Sir, if you don't want to put a label on a relationship, are you really saying the woman you're with right now is *off brand, generic—basic?* Are you saying she doesn't deserve a title, but you *do?*

The *title* identifies the brand, what is pictured on the logo. It is the image, the *vision* of what's supposed to be.

Woman: if he's saying, **I don't do labels,** he's means, "I do not want anyone to *identify* me or associate me with **you**." Women, you should never have to ask a man more than once, *"What is our relationship?"* You really shouldn't have to ask him even once. It is the man's responsibility to set Vision, and to set the *course* *and purpose* of the relationship. If he's not saying it, if he's not setting it, it's because he doesn't want to say it, he does not want to set it. He's not serious.

No real man wanders about not knowing what he's doing or with whom he's doing it? He has no plans? No understanding? That's either a boy or exactly the type of man you don't want. And don't buy the line that he's been hurt in the past, so he doesn't want to move too quickly. Then why does he quickly want you to provide him with things that only married men should be getting?

This man is to set order and be set in order with God so he can then set Vision and the Course for the relationship. If he's not, then you two are *not in a relationship.* You are not communicating. He's getting goodies from you and you're getting nothing –, you're in a **lay***sionship,,* there's no *re-* to it. He knows what your connection is and what he desires it to be. He just not willing to say it because the truth may not serve his purpose(s) right now.

Speaking of titles, you go to school for how many years to earn a degree? You go to school to earn a title. And you don't like it when people don't respect *your* title, or call you out of your name. Neither would any man, or a driven woman. A connection with intercourse, but no set course, no vision, no order, no title is a Sexual Wilderness where you shouldn't be.

Wilderness Man: she's not trying to trap you; she needs <u>information</u> to govern *herself* accordingly. She might want to stay, she might want to leave, but that may not suit your purposes right now. There is deceit here and it doesn't seem to be on her part.

Without a title your authority is compromised or non-existent. If you don't have authority to speak to a certain condition, situation or problem, you are helpless. And believe it, you will be told that more than once, in your "relationship" if you do not have a title, that you do not have position, standing, or right to speak to him like that, or to ask him *that.* He's really telling you that you are *Nobody* to him, yet your body is what he's after.

I'm talking a simple title of *girlfriend* or *fiancé* **with a ring and a date set**. The Wilderness Man can't set the course for a proper relationship because he's wandering around and around in the Wilderness himself; he's a Wilderness Man.

The Perpetual Test Drive

If that man is pretending to be *planning* to give you a title while he takes you out on a test drive, a *try out* for a relationship—don't fall for that. He may be pretending that he's planning to give you a title when that's not really the intention at all. Men test drive a lot of cars they have no intention of buying. This is a jr. high school, high school level game. If you fall for it and realize all he wants is sex… then you have to admit that you fell for it. He is just *sampling* you, for as long as you let him.

If that's you, you really need to read this book.

Committed to You

Men (and women) *can* commit to things all the time. Modern day: a man who goes into a car *dealership*, to buy a car knows that it's a car and what he's going to do with that car, where he will drive it and even how it will fit into his garage. This grown man knows the purpose of **everything** in his house, in his life, so why is a woman a nebulous thing that he's *confused* about or *non-committal* about? He doesn't know what kind of relationship you two are having, while *everything* in his house is **labeled.**

Oh please.

He committed to buying *that car,* detailing *that car,* getting all the tags, licenses, stickers and insurance for *that car. If he can do that for* an object, how much more for an actual living soul, a person, a woman. The point is that a man **can** commit to what he wants to commit to.

A man can commit. He can commit to a steak for dinner & knows if he wants it well done, medium, or medium-rare. He knows what he wants and how he wants it. Every day. Every night.

Committing is done verbally, but sometimes it's done non-verbally. That's why men act surprised by what the woman believes (knows) just happened between them by *what just happened between them*, whether words were involved, or not. A spiritually dull man does not know that sex with a woman means he just made a **covenant** with that woman. He's a dangerous man if he doesn't know that. He's even more dangerous if he knows it and pretends that he doesn't.

When this non-committal type man --, if he can't find what he thinks he is really looking for in a woman, or if he can't *attract* it – don't <u>you</u> try to make yourself fit what he's *saying* he wants. He may just be saying that *today*. That may be what he wants today. If he's noncommittal, he's non-committal, and he thinks he has the right to be this way. That's the world's dangerous game, not God's.

A fellow described the perfect woman to me once. when he was through talking, I asked him, *what would make a woman like that interested in you?* then he was really done talking after I asked that—because he realized he was living in fantasy land.

Now about this living, breathing, human being with a soul and a spirit? If he doesn't know what to do *with* you or *about* you, maybe he should <u>learn first</u>, then step to you.

Woman: You are not a doormat, a place holder or a proxy until the "real thing comes along." You're not in waiting while he decides *if* he wants you for real or not. If he hasn't already told you and it's been a minute already– move on. Real love will not make you wonder or be confused. A real man won't risk losing you. you are fearfully and wonderfully made. A real man won't risk losing real love by playing games.

He doesn't believe in titles. Really? He's Wilderness.

He has a job. Would he go to that job without knowing *his* job title? *His* position? *His* salary? *His* benefits? The *benefits package* is **completely** different for different job titles. A mailroom clerk has a different benefits package than a VP or the President of the company. He wouldn't work under those conditions, so why should **you** work *in* a relationship, *for* a relationship or *toward* a relationship where you don't even know what your title is or will be? Yet **he** wants the full *benefits package* with no title—yeah, he got angry because you called him your boyfriend? He's Wilderness.

Another Wilderness phrase: *Go with the flow.* What *flow?* Go with the flow means absolutely nothing.

Why should you work *in a relationship* with or for someone who doesn't, by his own admission, not know who you are? Or what your purpose is? What your value is?

Not knowing means he doesn't *care* to know – hasn't tried to know; he is wasting your time. Just because he wants to *waste his own time,* his health, strength, and resources doesn't mean that you should waste yours along with him.

47

Where and how you fit into his life, *if* you fit into his life, he knows the answers to the questions you have. But there you are waiting. Showing him how patient you are. Auditioning. Showing him how kind you are. You are requiring **nothing** of him, showing him how cool you are. You are not impressing him; you are the perfect patsy.

Don't you think you are a *valuable* and connecting with you in life is to both your advantages. He immediately knows where and if that car and that steak fit into his life and how often he wants to drive the car or have the steak.

Jesus thought you were worth it. He thought you were worth saving, worth redeeming. So, why can't the person who you want to be in relationship see your value? Most often this type reduces you to your wallet or the body parts he likes, as if you're a chicken three-piece meal.

What that Wilderness Man is looking to see if **you** know your value and how much you are willing to put up with. He knows how that car and that steak, how they will fit into his life. He knows. You have to value yourself.

My opinion: If a man hasn't stepped out of the *I'm confused, I don't know what we are doing phase*, in one to three months into the protecting, communicating, planning, setting vision for your relationship phase -- he's not planning to. He's most likely not planning to stay or step up. Pray and ask God.

He's not confused; he knows what he's doing. He just needs to tell you, but he doesn't want to risk losing the convenience of having you hanging around *for his convenience.*

Where's your power? Where's the part where **you** decide if this connection is working for **you** or not? Why so concerned about what *he* feels about you and about your relationship. If what he's offering is not enough for you, move on, you should walk away. Govern *yourself* accordingly. If it doesn't fit, don't force it.

Before he puts a ring on it, he will put a name on it. He **will** label it; he will give it a title and call it what it is, then he's for real.

Remember your worth, your value, your power. You don't have to overpower anyone but know who you are and what you are willing to accept and what you are not willing to accept. Talk to God about it. God will help you make your relationships work or advise and empower you to keep it moving. Sometimes when you are not being treated well, your silence is **<u>consent</u>** for the perp to keep doing what he's doing to you.

Do No Harm

One of the most dangerous things on earth is a **spiritually unprotected** person who either *thinks* he's protected, ***pretends*** he's protected, or doesn't have sense enough to know that he needs spiritual protection. The Wilderness person is one such individual. He wanders, roams, circles, and circles back again because he doesn't have God at the head. There are coyotes, hyenas, all kinds of danger in a wilderness, it's perilous but there he is roaming in it.

If you picked the entirely wrong person for a relationship, this chapter is for you. in such a case the most you may get is ***physicality***. That's it, and that's when he wants it and if he wants it. Often that's all he wants, to break and enter, to Pop A Lock. It's a game to too many. Most of the ones who are playing this game want the women who want to stay pure and virtuous. Playa's sometimes want to do it just once, just to say they *did*.

The woman is seeking companionship, will she get it that with one of these types? *Probably not.* Where is he? She doesn't know most of the time. He might roll through on occasion, but he will want to know where you are 24/7.

She might want some fun; will she get any? Don't know. There will probably be a lot of arguing. *"Where were you, why didn't you call me? We had plans, why didn't' you come by?"*

He might respond, *"You have no right to ask me that, you aren't my girlfriend or nothing like that."*

Physical Protection, will there be any? Maybe. But if he's not consistent in talking with you, checking on you, he might not give a care if you are safe or not. If he's a coward, he might expect you to protect *him* instead of the other way around.

In a relationship a woman might want Financial Stability. Don't get me started on this. There are those who **have** and don't share. There are those who have and still want to take yours while they keep theirs. There are those who don't have but pretend they do. There are those who don't have and expect you to help them out and raise them up. You decide what's the right relationship for you. It should be **none** of the above.

What should not be expected, people of God, women especially, is for that person to bring spiritual disorder or disaster to you. Men want to be the leader; he's supposed to set the course for the relationship not set the **CURSE** for the relationship. The relationship should not be cursed. Do No Harm!

Soul Problems

We should be helping one another prosper and grow our souls. If he's been out cavorting and meeting challenges that his bro's set up for him, he might be **soul tied like a mug**. You've kept yourself pure while he's been out there in the field, sowing his wild oats, out in the *field*, getting spiritual dirt all over himself, wallowing in a Sexual Wilderness.

He comes in tracking up the house. He shows up bound and soul tied. What do you think he can do for <u>your soul</u> when **NO part of his soul is even available** for a relationship? Iron could be sharpening iron if he was available for the relationship. Is he emotionally available? Probably not.

Emotionally unavailable?

Physically available? No.

Intellectually available? Do you two talk about anything of any importance? Do you talk about real life and godliness?

He doesn't *get over* things/hurts easily? Ever?

He's soul-tied? **N**ow you have to date the last person he was in a relationship with. Worse, he might **still** be in relationship with _____, because he's lying to you. Or he's still in relationships with **everyone** he's ever been in a relationship with because he forgives nothing and holds on to everything.

Do No Harm – anything that is not prospering your soul is interfering with your soul's growth. It is interfering with God's plan for your life.

Ladies, anytime you've got to sit around alone or with friends and try to figure out why, why, why? Why did he do this or that? What is he doing? What does this mean? Why is he vague? <u>He **is wasting your time**</u>. If he's inconsistent, *he's wasting your time*. If he's not definitive about your relationship *he's wasting your time*. If you're young, he's wasting your youth and your time. If you're not young, he's *wasting your time. Both golden years and youth are precious and should not be wasted.*

This Wilderness man is bringing you spiritual problems because of all the **spiritual dirt** on him. Have compassion and pray for him until he can pray for himself. But don't waste your time trying to *fix* him.

Crazy, Spiritual Problems

Speaking of spiritual problems, is he's such a bad boy that he's an out-law with God???

Malachi 2:11 ... hath married the daughter of a strange god.

You'd better find out what **God** that person is serving—and who he's been married to or in alliances with **before** making an alliance with him. Who has he been with in the past? Is he still with them and what cross contamination, *spiritually* is he bringing into your life? What spiritual dirt is he dragging in from the **Wilderness, from the *world*?** The world that you are shunning, staying away from and trying to remain pure from. Why are you letting someone bring spiritual dirt to you?

In the natural is he bringing some **CRAZY** into your life? Is there some random chick in his past, or that he's still dealing with that is obsessed with him and is willing to blame you, obsess on you because he stepped out on her??? You'd better find out before you go any further.

Let's say you make that alliance with this person and all kinds of stuff starts happening to you and in your life – stuff you never experienced before. Is it him? Or is it the stuff that's **on** him from some unholy alliance that he made with someone else who serves ***strange gods***?

You'd better ask God. Today would be a great day to do that. Things that are so strange that you've been turned into a spiritual profiler to pray about and discern and try to figure out *what is this attack that you're under? Where did it came from?* When you realize how spiritually weak that good looking, charming, good smelling fellow is – **PRAY for him. As they say on airplanes if the oxygen mask drops place your on first before trying to help another person. Prayer is an oxygen mask. If you're going through strange happenings in your life; the OXYEN MASK JUST DROPPED. Big time.**

You may think he's got it together because he looks good, smells good and talks *good*. He's got a job/career. And appears to be a grown up. So, you let your guard down because he's convinced you to be in a "relationship" with him. OMG! I seriously mean this.

Soul Snatching

Talk about damaging the soul. I want to talk about **soul snatching** – it *ain't* that – it's when somebody has got your mind. This blocks you from being able to conduct your own life. That's when your soul has been *snatched*. You need your own mind to conduct your life.

Nobody can just steal your soul. If you decided to not have spiritual protection because you're so big and bad and you don't believe in God? Don't pray? Don't fast? Don't praise or worship or obey the tenets of the faith as much as it's in you. Then that's a choice you've made. Nobody can steal your soul unless you are lawless, prayerless and careless, and especially if you were born into an evil foundation. You don't repent, don't renounce, you keep collecting Wilderness spiritual dirt everywhere you go. Your soul could be on the auction block.

Spiritual Dirt

But here's this good looking dude tracking in spiritual dirt from every spiritual Wilderness and spiritual pigpen he's ever been in – tracking it in from where he's been, along with all the **curses** that he's attracted to himself over all his years of attracting dirt.

You don't know what he's dragging into your life!

You don't know if what he's dragging into your life wants to drag you. Have you ever noticed that when you break up with a wrong person your life **suddenly** gets better? That's a sign of what pigpen you were in with him, what pigpen he brought you. Uh huh. Your life quickly gets better. God is the same way when you drop spiritual dirt, God blesses you.

In the natural, your dad, brothers etc. appreciate you again and start doing things for you that they had stopped doing for you because you *"have a man."*

The world opens up to you again. You get a new job that you didn't even apply for –or a promotion that you've been wanting for so long. You get a raise. A bill gets forgiven or mysteriously **paid**. A stranger pays for your gas on Pump 5.

You find a $10 bill on the sidewalk. Your clothes fit looser, and you weren't even on a diet.   You   are getting compliments everywhere on how nice your skin looks. You're glowing. You look so happy.

On TikTok they say, *You wake up in the morning and look in the mirror and even your teeth look whiter, and you haven't even brushed them yet.*

Friends start coming around again, saying we never liked him anyway. God's talking to you again. Well – you've started listening to God again. Listening to God rather than *that fellow*.

Yeah, you broke a stronghold over your life. You broke a *soul tie.* Now the blessings of God can flow to you again. Heaven above you opens again.   Oh   my God!!!

When the devil was kicked out of Heaven a third part of the stars fell with him, to Earth. There is no surprise that there **is** resident evil in the earth. A third part that were influenced by the devil – those who think all this is funny? Fun and games? A third part of *people* in the earth *may not be* relationship material at all? May not be so you can't just go by looks and natural senses.

- o   Is he cute?
- o   Is he a good dresser?
- o   Does he have a nice job/bank?
- o   Is he a good conversationalist?

We are not dating angels or fallen angels this talk is hypothesis. So, out of the 70% or so that are left who are not evil or pure evil, ½ of them might be the gender that you're looking for…So you see, indiscriminately looking for a partner/spouse is NOT an option; you've got to seek God and discern the spirits. Just anybody won't do.

Even if you're a good girl and he's a good guy, he's good looking and you're good looking, and you both agree on that and you're both very attracted to each other, but if you two have NO SPIRITUAL BUSINESS, NO PURPOSE together, you're not supposed to be together. *Periodt*. That doesn't mean that either of you are bad people, you just don't need to be together, you two have PURPOSE together and you'll be blocking two others from being with *their* right people.

Men: Vacillating from *it's all about me, all women should want me until I get the one or ones I want.* **To: *I want all Women, that's why I can't pick one;*** *it is all demonic.* You're wasting valuable time, energy, resources, and life on throw away things when you could be building your relationship, your future, your family, your family's future, your destiny, your legacy – instead of listening to a bunch of dumb unspiritual, ungodly guys who are influenced or oppressed by ungodly demons.

Temporary Marriage

Reiterating, one of the most dangerous things on earth is a spiritually unprotected person who either *thinks* he's protected or *pretends* that he is protected or doesn't have sense enough to know that he needs **spiritual** protection. We are spirits; we have souls, and we are having a flesh experience as we travel Earth. We need spiritual protection because *life is spiritual, says Minister Erica Shepherd.*

He Restores My Soul

We are charged by God to prosper in our souls, Beloved I wish above all things that you would prosper and be in health even as your soul prospers, (3 John 1:2). God restores our soul (Psalm 23:6). If God restores and wants our souls to prosper, then our souls should not be eroding, instead, we should be lifting one another up. We should be in relationships that **prosper in our souls**. If not we should have the power to pray and change things, or the Wisdom to break camp, and walk away.

We need spiritual and soul protection because enemies of God are after our souls.

None of us are perfect, as we go through life, we may experience mental exhaustion, downturns in emotions; our souls need restoration and renewal from time to time. God promises to restore our souls. As man is created in the image and likeness of God, we should be treated as God would treat us, or some facsimile of that by all other people, no matter what type of relationship. In an interpersonal relationship where you let someone into the most intimate parts of your life, that should be edifying connection, not one that tears you down.

Wisdom, show us when to pray and show us when to walk away. Amen.

Hopefully your soul should not need restoration, but if it does, that man should be part of your soul's restoration. At the very least, he should never be getting in the way of it being **restored**. He should never *cause* your soul to be eroded, deteriorated, or to become less than. He should never tear you down, he should always be building you up. He should never be breaking you down or doing any harm to you, or any harm to anyone's soul--, whether a friend, a loved one, or interpersonal relationship. Do not UN-restore any soul. Do not break it down. That is, he is to do no harm to another's soul:

- Emotionally.
- Intellectually.
- Do not break another's *will*.

Women are ever trying to restore a man's soul from his alleged past, that was so much more devastating and horrible than theirs. Why? I do not know because he was at least directing his own path, women are more often than not the would-be victims. But I say, don't fall for the okie doke as he pours out all the reasons why he can't commit in a relationship. If you really listen whatever is wrong with him, according to his own account is the reason why he can't commit to you.

Let him talk; you pray for ears to hear, Amen.

Men sometimes play a game where they try to talk women into physical things that they never should be talking them in to. That takes the breaking of the woman's **_will_**. She says, _No._ His tactics include trying to be more convincing, charming, cute. He has tactics, the devil has wiles; is there a difference? Listen closely to hear who is talking, him or his demons. Wisely, she says, "No," again.

Dude Pop A Lock is breaking the **_will_** of another human being so that he can have his way with her. That is EXACTLY the game!!! Urging. Coaxing. Convincing. Conniving. I am not saying this all happens in the same evening, or the same day, could be over weeks or months. He's trying to break and enter, pop-a-lock, like this is fun, trying to break this woman's **_will_**.

As the game goes, he will convince her, and she will believe that he is absolutely crazy about her and getting more crazy about her by the moment. What an ego trip for her! She feels the tug on her fishing line and believes she's got a keeper. Irony: He is reeling her in, not the other way around.

As her **will** is broken and she gives in, this is destroying her soul and putting her smack in the middle of a *Sexual Wilderness*. The emotions the intellect and will are part of the Soul. The man is to do no harm to a woman, to a woman's soul. Yet there he is trying and vying to break in, break her will by intimidating, manipulating. wooing. tricking. dominating--, by any means necessary.

A human should never leave another's soul in worse condition than he finds it. But most give no thought to another's soul other than if someone gets mad at them and for them to stop being mad at them. Most give no thought to another's soul.

A dude like this thinks he's dealing with **flesh, only flesh**. He may be a flesh creature and thinks everyone else is the same way. Especially *good church girls* who profess Christ but give in to him anyway. If he is not saved, not giving in to him is the only way he will see the difference between you and unsaved , and then respect you.

He thinks he's dealing with your flesh, but really, he's dealing with your **soul** *and* putting your spirit in jeopardy. This is a trauma to your **whole** soul, assuming it is whole when he met you. This begins the fragmentation of your soul and once divided, everything is easy to conquer--, even a soul. Trauma to an already fragmented soul makes it even easier for the devil to take it captive.

With God, in a Godly covenant is the only way you can make covenant with another and not jeopardize your soul. If you are having sex with someone you are not married to, the devil is in that connection, and he (most likely) sends demons <u>into</u> the sex act ***with you*--, even if you are by yourself, and especially if you are with another or others. Sex is the most common and easiest way to get demons into your life.

Mind blowing, highly spirited sex? Demons are most likely involved. Period. Best sex you ever had?

You're hooked on him? He's probably demonized. Come on, without pharmaceuticals a man can't last for 5 hours. Ten hours? Something is not human here.

The guy leaves: he leaves you *demons*.

You **stress** out, more demons come.

You **worry** about him, why hasn't he called? Where is he? More demons.

You face the truth; you've been used. Now you have **shame, embarrassment, sadness.** More demons.

Is there a pregnancy, an STD, or the **fear** of either? More demons.

You **hate** him--, more demons.

You hold **unforgiveness** toward him, more demons.

You move into **bitterness** and **resentment**? More demons.

You **grieve** the relationship, oops, I mean *situationship*, more demons arrive.

You find out he has a girlfriend, fiancé or a whole wife and kids--, or worse, 3 baby mamas! Now you have **rage** and want **revenge**: more demons enter.

Now you have compounded problems that must be solved all because you said, *Yes* when the answer was still, **NO**!

This line of conversation does not apply to anyone who was <u>forced</u> into the Sexual Wilderness. May the LORD restore and heal your body, soul and memory, in the Name of Jesus. Amen.

Criminal Negligence

God sees how this has damaged your soul. It is one of the reasons the Bible tells us NOT to do this. The Bible (God) is a *Because-I-Said-So* parent, because God's thoughts and ways are higher than ours and we might not understand the *whys* and why-nots of a hundred different things. We should just OBEY the Word, but too many times we humans ignore warnings and disasters result.

Before an airline pilot takes off, he is advised how many **souls** are on board. He is to safely bring those souls to the next destination. A cruise ship captain – same thing: how many souls are on board? He is also charged with bringing those souls safely back to harbor or to the appointed destination. If either captain doesn't fulfill the responsibility of bringing those souls safely to port again, they may face criminal charges. It is criminal to hurt, lose or damage another soul.

This is why the role of pastors is so critical. Pastors are the bishops of our souls. They have charge over our souls. God judges them differently. We need to know if we are supposed to be in a particular church or not, but God is the Righteous Judge.

Evil, selfish, childish, lying, immature, probably demonized men continue trying to break the will of women to have flesh pleasures with them. **They are promoting themselves as captain over a soul or souls where they have NO jurisdiction, no authority, no anointing, no good intention, no experience, no plans of nurturing, keeping, even offering protection or safety to**

the souls of the people whose bodies they defile. They themselves do not have spiritual protection and dare tread into the world of **souls and spirits** (via the flesh). They have given no thought to and do not care if they bring that soul back where and in the condition in which they found it.

There are those who dare to tread into the realm of souls and spirits and at least leave a soul neutral---, do no harm. They should have charged themselves to leave that soul better than they found it. There are criminal spiritual charges of dealing treacherously with the souls of people, especially God's people. One may feel like he got away with it because "nothing" happened. A lot happened to her and to him. The iniquity of the sin incurred from this treachery will pass on to his generations. He may think he's out here living life on his on terms; doing it his way when really, **he is living the lives of his children, grandchildren and great grandchildren.** Creating iniquity that will overtake them as soon as they are born, no matter how cute they are. This will all remain and be counted against him if he doesn't repent. Perhaps your ancestors did something similar; could be why you may have surprise spiritual problems.

Living as if life is a game is not wise. A dangerous, reckless, non-spiritual person with a scorch the Earth mentality, who plans to only live once is likely to play this game. No **soul** is a toy. No one's soul is to be played with. No one's soul is anything you ever want to damage or harm--, not anyone else's soul; and definitely not your own.

The devil comes to steal, kill & destroy – everything from flesh, to souls, to spirits – if he can. The man who wants to break the *will* of a woman is working for the dark side when he treats a soul this way. And what does he think the payoff is for doing this? Flesh? That's the payoff? More flesh? How can the devil promise you the FLESH of another person? How can a person presume to take the **flesh** of another human being *for their own use,* and indiscriminately thinking they'd never have to PAY for dealing ***treacherously*** with people-- especially God's people. He may exclaim, she agreed. She was asking for it. She came to my hotel room at midnight… *So if one of you is stupid, both are supposed to be stupid?*

Goes into equals married. *Goes into* forms SOUL TIES. The DEVIL is in every soul tie. A soul tie is the devil's counterfeit of God's marriage covenant. Souls are not designed to be TIED or BOUND. We came here as separate whole souls, and we are supposed to stay that way. Each of us **need our <u>whole</u> soul to worship and serve God and to fulfill our purpose in the Earth.**

To get unmarried in the natural requires a divorce. To get un-soul tied requires GOD because it's *the kind of connection that men put together. Soul ties can be broken because they are not of God.*

If you do not repent – what do you mean if *I* don't repent, exclaims the perceived victim. Woman: you've got to worry about yourself right now: if you don't repent and renounce, all these demons could get into your bloodline. As time keeps ticking, soon it will be time to pass the torch onto your next generation. Surely, this is not what you want to pass on to them the fallout of the sin acts that invited all these demons into *your* life?

Conversely if that man (and you) is living Godly lives, you are setting up blessings for your children, grandchildren and great grandchildren. Living well is not the best revenge, except against demons. Living GODLY is living well.

Incurring Curses

Destroying souls will curse you and it will land you on a sick bed or in your final years all alone because you didn't invest in your own future by investing in proper, Godly behavior and relationships.

Any woman is not made for every man. A man is not made for every woman. Trying to force it is stupid and a waste of all spiritual and physical effort. **It's also dangerous!!! If you get tied up with the wrong person who is not serving the Most High God and if you don't have spiritual protection, you could be in for a world of hurt.**

Women, just because he's paying you lots of attention –today, doesn't mean that he's **the one**. He could be an actor, or on a mission. He could be a plant sent by the devil to derail your plans and purposes. He could look and smell amazing, but *who* is he? **Who is he worshipping in his life**? What *god* is he serving? What altar does he bow at? You'd better learn today. Satan can turn himself into an angel of light; most elect of God, do not be deceived.

Men if you are dealing treacherously with women, you are at extreme risk. Men, for your information there are women, no matter what they look like that you should not involve yourself with in any way. The enemy sends in **exactly** what you want a woman to look like, be like, walk or talk like. You'd better *discern every spirit*. You've seen her. There she is. Should you proceed? Better ask God. Else you may be left in shambles.

for Judah hath profaned the holiness of the LORD which he loved, and hath married the daughter of a strange god. Mal 2:11

Men, you'd better find out what *god* your chosen *"temporary wives"* are serving. Loose women, those who **say** they serve God--, which *god?* Need to know before you make an alliance with them. The fallout, the spiritual dirt of what you do with or to a woman could follow you for decades. She, and the people who are with her--, relatives, friends, **covens**-- may be waiting to heap it on you for what you did to her, or even what she *thinks* you did to her. Depending on what *god* they serve, they may think anything goes. Depending on what God you serve, and if spiritual protection, you may survive their plans and spiritual attacks. Make sure it is the Most High God, Jehovah.

You have spiritual protection if you practice the disciplines of the faith; you are not prayerless, careless, or rebellious.

Legacy

Men and aggressors, in your later years, if your memory serves you may think of all the things you did to get over on one unsuspecting woman (person) after another as you think over your whole life. You will have to give account for every deed and every word spoken. You will. We all will.

True story: I know a man just past mid-life who has lost a lot of his mental capacity and memory. What he does remember, and only what he remembers is the sexual escapades of his youth. He is permanently stuck in a Sexual Wilderness, that he can't act out, and doesn't even have enough sense to know it's a curse and he's being tortured with those memories. I personally think it's witchcraft and have sent word to him of the same. Perhaps you as the reader will avoid such, even though this man and the people around him aren't able to hear what the Spirit is saying to get him delivered and back in his right mind again.

Men, choose wisely, especially in your youth. **Do no harm** to others, especially to women that **you're put here to <u>protect</u>**. Especially God's women. God will judge you harshly if you've dealt treacherously with women, His women especially.

The trap you set for others will be the one that gets you. When you have children, your daughter will bring home a man just like you, it's all she's seen. That will certainly be a curse. Don't think you've hidden it; everyone knows, they are just not saying anything or have wearied of begging you to change. Your darling daughter will bring home a Wilderness man, unless you repent or she with God, by the Blood of Jesus takes a different course--, out of the Wilderness.

Sometimes the hunter does get captured by the game and the game ain't playing. Sometimes that alluring, beautiful creature that you shouldn't even be out in the streets looking for, is drawing you, pulling you, and maybe your downfall. Why do it, when you've got the real thing at home, the real thing that you prayed for; sent by God? Don't deal treacherously with that gift from God. And even if you think you want strange – let's put it this way, *Strangerous can be very Dangerous.*

Sometimes that alluring, beautiful creature is a creature, a plant of the enemy to actually CAPTIVATE you, trap you, derail you, or take you down. You have to try every spirit!!! And you'd better know what spiritual practices that alluring beautiful creature is practicing, dabbling in –, and their momma, and their auntie and their daddy and granddaddy – all down their family line. You may not ever get out of that Hotel California. And, if you do, they may have put every curse on you that they know.

No curse can alight without a cause; the curse, causeless cannot alight, (Proverbs 26:2). But if you are not spiritually protected, it's open season, Bruh. Make no mistake, when you step out of the will of God into sin, fornication, adultery, and other sins, spiritual protection is gone. Period.

No one can curse what God has blessed. Spiritual protection is a blessing of God. No man can bless what God has cursed. Be wise; make sure that every choice you make makes a positive difference in every tomorrow. Don't throw away your legacy by showboating in front of your boys. None of yo' boys have a heaven or a hell to put you in.

Keep your own Legacy in mind.

Put Her Away

In the Bible and also now men have been *"putting women away"* or trying to put them away. In the Sexual Wilderness, when playa is through with a woman, he's ready for her to just **go away.** In the times of Moses women lost their **lives** dealing with men who were prone to *"put them away"*. So God said, **Stop killing your wives (just because you want a new one) and give them a divorce. God does allow divorce.**

Dating a divorcee? Marrying a divorcee does **not** mean you will be committing adultery, as long as any party who has been maried before has a **real** divorce. The Law of Moses commanded divorce for **neglect, or abuse,**

physical or emotional. The Law of Moses actually **commanded** divorce for breaking any of the three marriage vows in Exodus 21:10: **food, clothing, and "marital rights," which can be defined as** *love,* as we read in the New Testament: .

> *If he takes another wife to himself, he shall not diminish [the first wife's] food, her clothing, or her marital rights. And if he does not do these three things for her, she shall go out for nothing, without payment of money.*
> *Exodus 21:10-11 (ESV)*

That's hair, nails and money for new clothes, people. If he doesn't do these things for her, she can divorce him.

In the NT Jesus specifically allowed divorce for **infidelity:** *And I say to you: whoever divorces his wife, except for sexual immorality, and marries another, commits adultery* (Matthew 19:9 ESV). This is where the misspoken, misinterpreted scripture comes from. If the divorce is for anything other than infidelity, then that is adultery for the one that remarries. Stands to reason. God hates idolatry which is cheating on God...

Apostle Paul allowed divorce for **abandonment:** Some people honored giving a proper divorce, some did not but instead *"put their wives away".* (1 Corinthians 7:14-15 NIV).

In life it seems a woman has stricter rules than a man, then and now. A woman has to remain virtuous to be "wife material." All the while men could pretty much do whatever they want. Who were they doing this whatever *with?* Dunno—, you tell me. Also men did not have to remain virtuous to be "husband material." Women have to remain *pure.* So the woman's job was to fight off:

- Men – who were stronger than her.
- Men who have more money/power than she had. She had to fight the ME-TOO's of her day all by herself, even against a rich/powerful man to keep a job she really needed to keep.
- Her own feelings/emotions to stay pure.

- Her own needs (because only men have needs. Only men have libido? This is ludicrous. This is the ultimate in narcissism – when one believes that **_their_** needs are the only ones that are important or real.

And remain pure so a man who may or may not be pure himself, will **want** to marry her. Oh yeah, and she had to remain *pure* **while** married so the man doesn't just wake up one day and decide to *put her away*. If she was considered impure, corrupted or adulterous in any way, a man could just *"put her away"* and be done with the "marriage". *Shalach (Hebrew)* and (Greek), *apoluo* are translated '*put away*'. Both of those words are used for the **husband who can just orally** dismiss his wife of any length of marriage and send her away *without* a divorce decree. There was no court or judge involved, the man just spoke to his wife. Or probably yelled at her, *"Get out! And take these kids with you."* There, all better.

Putting away is not an official divorce. Most of the time it didn't need to be because the people involved were already previously married and *unofficially* married again. Shacking up is nothing new. Still, women and her children could have been stoned to death for having been *put away*. That would be the end of that, except for the curses of bloodshed on the land which is another whole book.

Laws of Sexual Morality

Deuteronomy 22:13 allows a man to marry, *go into* the woman, hate her and then **put her away**. Of course, spirit spouse may make him hate her. How? Spirit spouse gives inklings, ideas, thoughts, tells a man everything that's wrong with that woman. Tells a woman everything that's wrong with her husband. Each will think those are their own thoughts and each will feel so clever to see this in their natural spouse. But it's not that, it's spirit spouse.

Modern day: when a male decides that he's going to *pop that lock*, break into a place where he has no business, then putting away is the easy out to his inconvenient mess he's created, even though a whole covenant has been made. Hey, at least, in *some countries*, nobody will be stoned to death. *Putting away* is not even the dignity of a proper divorce, it's shaming, setting aside, rendering the woman and her offspring as second, or third-class citizens, used up and rubbish. The ultimate is condemnation which comes before destruction.

In the Bible a man could marry a woman and the next day decide she didn't *please* him. He could send her back to her folks, used, no longer a virgin. If she's been *put away*, she could be stoned to death for that, and he'd keep the dowry. So Old Testament, so ID Discovery.

What would happen to that man if the situation was reversed? Nothing. In Deuteronomy 22:28, there's precedent for all kinds of relationship scenarios. The shot gun wedding was a thing in the Bible before the shotgun was ever invented. The man would have to pay a dowry and marry her, and never be able to divorce her.

...and she shall be his wife because he has humbled her; he shall not be permitted to divorce her all his days.

Goes Into Equals Married

We can suppose the shotgun wedding had to be a thing because men's hearts are evil. In the Bible, *goes into equals married*.

But there are people, who are using the **God doesn't do divorce** excuse to justify why they are <u>not</u> committing to the divorced woman they've been seeing forever…as if a divorced woman is a non-person. If God doesn't allow divorce, which he does -- then that man -, and the woman are each **still married** to the first person they had *relations* with. The first person he *went into, unless that first person has died, is his spouse.* And so the next one and the next one. Sex contracts are messy. Blood/DNA are exchanged in the sex act. Contracts are struck and covenants are made.

God doesn't like divorce, but He does *allow* divorce. So a divorced man and a divorced woman both become **Singles** again. Let's get that right.

The New Testament says that deacons and church leaders should be husbands of **one** wife. This was written in the time when men could have *multiple* wives. It doesn't mean that he could have only married once, it means he *currently* does not have more than one wife.

Genesis Chapter 38: Tamar's first husband, Er was wicked so God killed him. Onan's dad told him to *go into* & marry Tamar (Onan's brother's widow) and Onan half obeyed and half disobeyed. Onan *went into* but he didn't commit. So God killed Onan. The point is that *going into, and marrying* are tied together, but Onan wanted the pleasure without the responsibility and so today goes the unsaved, ungodly, basic male. He's not more clever than the Bible people, that God killed.

Some Ways Covenant is Made

Eating together, the prophets that ate at jezebel's table. Drinks. Sex.

Pop A Lock

When a male decides that he's going to take his Bruh's challenge and *conquer* a woman to prove he's a man, or *the* man what he has really decided to do is *temporarily* marry that girl with plans to **abandon** her after he gets what he wants, or as much as he wants. In the natural, to set this up, he has to list his situation before the fake relationship starts. Here are some common set ups:

- His grown and gone kids keep him so busy.
- His kids always come first. (Nobody says otherwise.)
- He works long hours; he's always tired and not always available.
- He has so much on his plate.
- He travels a lot for work.
- He is an upstanding citizen, important to the community. He's a pillar of society and there for is *very importantly busy.*
- He's a good guy, almost a superhero. So many people need him.
- He's very important in his church. (Unspoken: he is willing to *temporarily* marry somebody, as long as he thinks nobody will know.)

God knows. Anyway, he's got all that said, now just a few more lies to set this whole thing up. Then the gaslighting--, he comes on like a ton of bricks, breaking down her soul making her think she is the reason he is living, until he closes the *deal*, then the breadcrumbing, or crickets or he completely ghosts her getting super busy in one of the aforementioned excuses.

This is cruel and demonic. God wouldn't even do this to the worst sinner. But now woman, you've made covenant with a person who has made himself into your enemy and an enemy of God.

That fellow took his home boy's challenge and in so doing he is saying, *"I'm going to sacrifice that girl. She is not my label anyway. She's not my kind. She's not my type. She's nobody. She's not important, like I am. She won't tell; no one will believe her anyway, not over me. She's not good enough for me, but she's good enough for right now."*

He indicates that he's willing to sacrifice her flesh and her soul and damage her or even completely break her spirit and leave her on the sidelines of life.... for dead.

He doesn't look back. It doesn't matter if someone picks her up or not. He got what he wanted.

This is far more serious than sacrificing a girl's or a woman's virtue, dignity, honor, position in society. He is sacrificing her future for this Bruh Challenge, for right now, for his pride and his physical pleasure. **What is done to the body has spiritual and soulish consequences.**

Ladies: do not allow yourself to be sacrificed on anyone's evil sexual altar. Maintain your purity, and virginity, pureness of spirit with an undamaged soul. Do not let your soul be wasted on toxic male challenges and foolish frivolity.

That male might be saying, *"I'm going to do whatever I have to convince her to do what I want, I'll say anything, even **temporarily marry her** (for tonight) and then put her away right after, or in the morning."* That is for those who make it to morning. No, I'm not going all ID Discovery on y'all today, just don't allow yourself to be sacrificed.

He's not thinking of the harm he is doing to her **soul** or even thinking she has a soul--, just flesh and also, he's ultimately doing harm to his own soul. Leaving either or both of them in shambles, making so much work for God to restore them. He doesn't see her as a soul. He's not a real Captain of anything, not of a plane, not a ship, not a Captain of his own destiny. He doesn't take proper care his own soul, so it's no surprise that he doesn't care for the soul that he's planning to put his hands on, the soul that he has no authority to touch. The soul he plans to defile.

Did the Tables Turn?

He has objectified her, making her into an object, discounting or denying that she has a SOUL or a spirit. She is God's property! He's not even thinking of his own soul, just his FLESH, pride, and ego AT THE Moment. He's not thinking the consequence of sin to his own soul either, else he wouldn't proceed with this. He may think he's doing something TO her, but what if she actually has plans and the ability to turn the tables on him? **What if she's serving strange *gods*?**

Men who selfishly think that only men have needs--, the ultimate in narcissism – when one believes that THEIR needs are the only ones that are important or real, beware. The tables can turn. The warning is here for men who are not spiritually protected, and they meet up with a human agent of the devil, who by all means is probably gorgeous. She might be your downfall.

In our society if women were taught the same as men to *hit it and quit it* all the time, what type of society, or civilization would we have? Yeah, I'm saying we'd have no polite society if everyone was a heathen.

If women are to remain "pure" and suppress their own libido, why don't men have to do the same? You don't know how difficult it is for any woman to keep her own flesh under control. Why do you think women eat so much??? We're working hard to stay *pure.* Those sandwiches, that ice cream is good. In the natural, food has not yet been outlawed, although the Bible says not to be given to appetite.

Most women are fighting to remain "decent" by societal, if not Biblical standards.

Why do men think it's not their own responsibility to "control" themselves and not deal treacherously with women?

A Pregnancy

In the mix of all of this, **she** gets pregnant. He says, his momma says, and society says she **trapped him**. Did she? *He* was the one who was out hunting and looking to trap someone. So the birth control is her responsibility also when she was saying NO, and she was saying NO, and she was saying NO, and she didn't even want to have sex with that guy? This makes no sense.

What are the man's responsibilities in a relationship again? He's supposed to be the leader and the ***protector*** of women. Adam said, *"God, that woman you gave me."*

In this case God can say, **"No son, It wasn't Me. I didn't *give* you a woman – you stole that one." Tricked that one. You lied to that one.**

Spiritual protection and a general upgrade or uptick in all areas would be expected if you are embarking on a relationship with somebody, else why would you get into a relationship with anybody? You both should be lifting each other up. This is true of a man, but it is also expected of a woman. Most women go into relationships optimistically, expecting better, an upgrade. Else, why do it?

Men, what do you think you're doing TO or FOR God's women when you get into these relationships with them? Spiritual protection would be expected—what if you don't know what that is, or can't even do it for **yourself, spiritually**? Then, are you *ready* for a relationship? Especially one that is long term that leads to marriage and children that also need upbringing and physical and spiritual protection.

We are spiritual beings having a flesh experience. Not the other way around. **We are NOT merely flesh beings who occasionally have a spiritual experience, like once a week on Sunday.**

Sexual Wilderness

As a warning to both ladies and gentlemen, a Wilderness person who has and is playing the field may be overloaded with demons that are *spiritually transferred*. Additionally, he or she may be *married in the spirit* to a **spirit spouse** and not even know it. The female spirit spouse (succubus) doesn't deal with the male the way the male spirit spouse (incubus) deals with the female human. So the male swears he doesn't have a spirit spouse.

The female human is more likely to know that something is wrong, or different, even if she doesn't know what a spirit spouse is. Let me say, do you wake up with marks, scratches and bruises on you? Spirit spouse. Do you have sex in the dreams with known or unknown people? Spirit spouse. Do you wake up aroused? Spirit spouse. Do you wake up in physical ecstasy? That wasn't a freebie, that was spirit spouse. Some women find actual fluid deposits and have mysterious infections when they are not even sexually active in the natural... spirit spouse.

Do your relationships that look promising from the start fizzle out for no reason? Spirit spouse. Does your natural spouse suddenly find you uninteresting or repulsive? Suspect spirit spouse – your spirit spouse or his spirit spouse – you both could have one **or more**. Do you feel like there is a ring on your ring finger, but there is no ring there? Spirit spouse is a demon, and it thinks it's married you. Somewhere in your dream life you may have been tricked into an evil satanic marriage. Spirit spouse.

A spirit spouse could have come down a person's bloodline, which might not be a surprise given the amount of lust your rolling stone ancestor could have been in. A spirit spouse could come from sexual transference of demons and one or more of those transferred demons opened the door to spirit spouse. It could have come from a jilted, lover who deals in black arts may have *sent* spirit spouse. OR, by your own sinful actions, you may incur a spirit spouse. For example, there is a **fantasy spirit spouse**. Movies, sex toys, make believe, masturbation, pornography and conjuring, you could be inviting all kinds of demons into your sex life. Don't do it!

The succubus is more subtle and probably gives pleasure to the male human. He thinks he's dreaming, but it is real sex. Adolescents who have wet dreams.... that's not a coming of age, that's spirit spouse. The human male has normalized this activity, it feels good and he's proud of it.

Incubus can be violent and possessive especially against any male paramour she may have. There are more than 30 different kinds of *spirit spouse.*

I've saw a spirit spouse in a vision while at my friend's house I had fallen asleep on his couch (not boyfriend because of the No Label thing. Yeah, I teach real stuff in my books.) Thinking I was dreaming, I forced myself awake and I still sensed her presence and heard her in the spirit boasting, *"He doesn't want you; he wants me. He's not staying here with you; he's going with me."*

Whoa!

I could share other stories of women being attacked by the man's incubus, but that same demon doesn't bother him, she just collects *seed* from him. Yes, to create spirit children. There are not enough pages in this book to tell all of spirit spouse and spirit children. To get more, research it yourself. On the Dr Miles YouTube channel find teachings on Spiritual *Spouse* and also, *People's Children*, with warfare prayers.

I also know of people who have been fasting, praying and resisting for **years** and still are awaiting and/or working toward deliverance as those demons can be stubborn. Nothing is too hard for God, so there are ways to get rid of them permanently.

Spirit spouse is the deepest depth of the Sexual Wilderness.

Promises, Potential, & More Promises

When God says He has a man for you, an Adam, go to the Scriptures and see what that is. An Adam is one who is:

- o Created and formed by God.
- o Under God's authority.
- o Has relationship with God.
- o Communes with God daily.
- o He is all grown up.
- o He has responsibilities and carries them out.
- o He walks in dominion and authority.
- o He's successful. That means he works.
- o And the woman is presented to him.

Every woman that was loved and adored of men, especially in the Bible, was sent for and *presented* to the man. She was protected, given gifts of appreciation and engagement. She was served, and she prepared herself to meet her husband. Eve was not dancing at a strip club until her fiancé came along. Rebecca was not working as a cocktail waitress. Mary, the mother of Jesus, was not a nightclub hostess. These women weren't scoping out guys in the clubs and bars looking for eligible men. BUT GOD can redeem any of us. All of us. Even the chief sinner among us all.

If you were not sent for, prepared, and presented, no wonder what happened, happened. We cannot apply Scriptural rules if you are not sent for, prepared, and presented. You cannot apply Scriptural rules to ungodly situations. You cannot expect the outcome that Christians get to be yours if you are not saved, born again baptized, Spirit-filled, and obedient. To think so is foolishness.

God had Hosea to marry a harlot, to prove a point. If you've been playing the harlot to win a man, then you will get a *whoremonger* as a mate unless God sends a Hosea to marry you. And if you've been playing the harlot, unless God sends a decent man to you, the man you connect with will also be a whoremonger. Whoremongers are not dependable, reliable, or anything else good. They are subject to treat you badly, or even abandon you, with or without children, to serve you their own desires and lusts. That lusting man is not lusting *just* for you.

Lust basically has no taste.

One day, I tried to get a friend, Dee to stop waving at men who honked their car horns as we walked along the shops, downtown Why? She had to know. I said, "*Listen.*" As she did the same car horn that had blown at her, turned the corner and blew at another pedestrian. She realized then that what she had been receiving as a compliment was no compliment at all.

Don't rush. And don't rush him. A butterfly out of season is a caterpillar. Wait a few seasons for him to come out of his cocoon and try out his wings. Don't be mad at the man because he's a caterpillar. If he's not ready; he's not ready. And you can't be mad at a man for being a creep, if he's a caterpillar he cannot fly; they creep.

If the season for metamorphosis has passed and he's not yet a butterfly, but still a creep, you have **my** permission to break camp and leave. But don't go anywhere until you check with God. I am not the Acknowledger and Director of your Paths; God is (Proverbs 3:6).

He's In Your Words!

Oh, but where is your mate?

Have you tried looking in your heart? Or in your conversation? Consider what you are saying. If you are prophesying doom and gloom over your romantic life, then that's what you'll get. If you are prophesying loneliness, singleness, and an unfulfilling life, that's what you'll get. I know. I did it, not out of despair or depression, but to be funny. But, funny, **it was not.**

When I got what I said, which was something I really didn't want, funny was not the adjective best suited to describe it. If you are prophesying by constantly reporting the negative type of man that you attract, that's what you will continue to attract; I know, I did it.

Change your conversation. It may sound odd the first few times you hear yourself, but if you continue to talk about how bad the men are that you meet, or are attracting or who find you interesting, you'll keep attracting those types. I know, I did it for years!

God has made someone for you. On this planet of billions and billions, surely God did not forget you. If He did, then you can get away with sinning. And you, with sinning, can't. So that proves it. He has got His eye on you.

And God said, Let us make man in our image, after our likeness... So God created man in his own image, in the image of God created he him; male and female created he them. (Gen 1:26-27)

There is someone for you. If you believe in the Creation, then for every man, God made a woman. Not only did He make a woman for each man; He made a man first, then He made you.

and the rib, which the Lord God had taken from man, made he a woman, and brought her unto the man.

(Gen 2:22)

After God made the woman, he brought her, **presented** her to the man. You don't have to go out into the night life looking for a man. First of all, you're not supposed to be looking for a man. If God has placed your man in a bar, or a dance club, you've got an unenviable problem. If you meet him there that's where you'll find him with regularity, with or without you. God has not placed Godly men in ungodly places to find Godly mates. So, get out of the ungodly places. God also has not placed Godly men in ungodly places for you. Instead, if you are sent to ungodly places, your job is to go in and evangelize. If you have an evangelism gift, praise God! Let's say you do win a soul to Christ, does that mean marry him? I don't believe that God called you to go get your husband and clean him up. There is no Biblical precedence of a woman being sent to get a man and fix him up to become her husband. Not one.

In Hollywood movies, but not the Bible.

Ladies, if you are more spiritually advanced than your man, he may feel intimidated, and insecure in your presence. How can he be the spiritual leader if you are? It takes an exceptional man to enter into that type of relationship successfully. That doesn't mean that if you are more spiritually advanced, you can't be friends (or more) with someone who just got saved. But wait on the right season. That season being when he realizes and at least begins to move toward the spiritual and other potential that God meant for him. If you're a college coed spiritually, how will you communicate daily with a spiritual kindergartener, without both of you becoming frustrated?

When a man meets a young lady, if she is not suitable, he moves on. WHY can't women learn that? My spiritual brother, David, is *"Ever amazed at the generosity of womenfolk."* You make the inference here.

Women fall in love with promises and potential. But when it comes to God can they believe God at His Word? If God says, "*I have a husband for you*, what do you do? You go try to find him yourself, bombarding God with questions like, *What does he look like? How tall is he? Where does he live? Where does he work? How much money does he make? Do I already know him, or is it someone I haven't yet met?* Then you go out and try to make a relationship happen. That's what you do on God's promise.

If someone did that to you in the natural, you wouldn't like it, would you? It sounds like you're interviewing God to decide if who God has for you is OK or not. God said, *I have a husband for you.* He didn't say, *I have three or four guys for you to pick from.* This is not a dating game. Is God's choice for you an option, or not?

Your choice was voiced when you:

- Prayed for and about a mate/husband.
- And when, every time you <u>spoke</u> about a mate.

- You have designed your mate by your prayers balanced with your words sent out to find mate. That is the only way you should go looking for a man, with your words. **Send your words out to heal your singleness**.
- Use Godly words or the devil will hear and be authorized to get what you **don't** want as a mate.

On God's Word, you go out and make a relationship happen on your own.

On a man's **promise**, such as, *"Honey, I'm going to get a job."* You say, "Okay" and keep working your fingers to the bone for 10 more years, paying all the bills yourself. Some of you even marry these promises and wonder why they are never fulfilled. You marry a man who's barely crawling, and you wonder why years later, your relationship, especially finances are still only crawling.

One thing about the average man, if he has nothing to lose, he sees no need to change; he will not change. You want a good man, and he wants a virtuous and good woman. You're keeping your end of the deal and the truth is, if you married him prematurely, before he had his own thing, and was the president of it, he's keeping his end of the deal, too. You still have just what you married.

Oh, you want to argue that you married him because he *promised*. True, he did. But you still don't have any less than you married. If you were marrying the future him, you married him too soon. If you wanted what he was promising in the future, right now, you married hm in the wrong *now*. You should have waited. If he's for you, he's for you. Nothing can change that, not time or a few seasons.

Or maybe you do have less. Since you've married him, he' s suddenly *retired*. That can happen. One Friday he came home and said that a woman got promoted over him at the job, and he was not going to work for her because she was dumber than he was (is that a compliment?). Anyway, by 11:00 am Monday morning, he's back home, hiding all his pension and retirement papers in his briefcase. He's not ashamed of his pension, as a matter of fact, he's rather proud of it because it's substantial. He just doesn't want **you** to see it. He's planning to tuck it all away for himself. Even though he boldly quit the job in a fit of pride, he's afraid that he won't get another one, or have enough money to live on. He's insecure now, added to being greedy, selfish, and misogynistic – bet you didn't know, did you?

He thinks the retirement money is not for you; it's only for *him*. He's a Wilderness Man. In reality, you're his wife, you can have HALF, right now. Once he's withdrawn it, half of it is yours; the same goes for *your* retirement fund.

Careful, that's another kind of ***right now*** that can lead to a financial Wilderness.

Surprise! Surprise! Surprise! You married a man who had not so much as missed a day from work, not even a sick day in 12 years of working for the same company and then within a year of being married to him, he suddenly quits his position at that company. Excuse me, retired. At age 40 he retires and has no other job opportunities, or ideas, and is not looking.

You prepared yourself and waited and prayed and held out for *this*? God you may ask, When do I get to hear the punch line, because this is a joke, right?

Well, you kept your end of the deal, even though you feel as though he didn't. But isn't that just like God? Doesn't God keep His end of the deal when we mess up, make a mistake, or move in rebellion? So, are you supposed to put up with this? I don't know. But consider Whose you are, and what He would do. Most of all, trust God and do what God says do, while moving in discernment. Say what God says about your personal life and situation. But if Mr. Wilderness disguises himself as a Promised Land Man, eyes and ears open--, you have to hear from God so He can direct you. Always remember WHOSE you are.

Men At Work

Searching for a mate is the man's job. Along with taking out the trash, washing the car, mowing the lawn, and opening doors for you. At least that's the stuff that a lot of women want men to do in a relationship. When you go out looking for a man, generally you find someone whom *you will be expected to do these things for*. Because that's how you'll attract him and win him. In addition to all those things, you will also be expected to do all the things that a woman is supposed to do too.

When a man sees that you will pursue him, it changes the entire spiritual makeup of the relationship or potential relationship. Being the pursuer puts you in a masculine energy. It makes him all *girly*. Is that what you want? You've just changed things that God had never intended to be changed. It usurps his manhood and his masculinity. Even if a man doesn't grab his manhood doesn't mean that his manhood is up for grabs. Another man can't take it, and a woman shouldn't try. The Jezebel-Ahab dynamic comes to mind.

That man may get into a pattern of waiting for you to call him, which is completely unnatural for a man. It should be for you too. He waits to see what you will to do next to win his favor. After all, the first stunt you pulled was pretty good. Women who pursue men become entertainment for them. It becomes fun for men, something to do, not to mention the ego trip they get because of it.

Too many get into so-called relationships in this way. After the relationship begins, the woman expects the roles to immediately reverse and for him to do the pursuing. This is not the Bugs Bunny Show; this is your real life. Do you seriously expect him, like some daffy cartoon character, to forget *you* were chasing **him** with flowers, cologne and dinners out? Do you think he'll easily forget the expensive gifts? Do you expect him to remember that he did all that for you instead of the other way around, the way it really happened? What would that even be called? Reverse amnesia? It won't happen. Step out of the twilight zone. Don't pursue the man. Appreciate him, but don't pursue him.

Now, especially off limits on the list of men to chase are Men At Work. Men who are on their jobs working are not at work to date. If you try to date on the job, you are revealing your reason for being there. Or it speaks of the men who are in the workplace, who are also not there to work. The latter you do not want as a potential spouse if the former applies, then you're violating this rule and you become the topic of much adolescent-like Wilderness Locker room or water cooler talk.

If this conversation seems worldly, it's because we are in the world. We are not supposed to be *of* it, being saved but in the world five and a half days a week, there will be challenges. The world's course is the one we navigate the most. Everybody at church *ain't* even a saint, so as we live, we must walk by the Spirit. Even if I see you at church every Sunday and Wednesday, I cannot give you a saint status the other five and a half days, unless it's revealed by the Spirit. Then your Christian status must be revealed by your Christian behavior. You've got to show it and live it, don't I?

If you think that's something, look where we're going now. Men At Work especially include men in the public eye, men in public places, and especially folk with a little or a lot of notoriety or celebrity. Just because you have a crush on, let's get real here, a certain pro basketball player and travel to every game he's in does not mean that he will be your husband. It does not mean that once he sees you or meets you that he'll be swept off his feet. I appreciate your self-confidence if you can call it that. **No.#** 1, you are not supposed to be sweeping him off *his* feet.

No# 2. Even if the man on the basketball court is a pro basketball athlete. playing a game, he's still a Man At Work. The man is doing his job and a very strenuous job it is.

No# 3. Even though he may be looking around or turning because of distractions toward loud noises or screams, it doesn't mean that you're the one. If you're one of the screamers that you've captured his attention, it doesn't mean that you will meet him, or that he will call you.

No# 4. After the game, even if he looks you straight in the eye, smiles and says, *"Hi,"* it doesn't mean that you two will date--, even if you call the team office repeatedly and leave your phone number.

Even if you are close enough to smell what The Rock is cooking, and you really admire the persona that his wrestling manager or publicist have created for him. Just because you come to the event all dressed up and smelling good and scream his name throughout the arena doesn't mean--, well, anything. The Man is At Work, he's doing his job. Just because you wear a low-cut blouse, and tight, tight clothes. Whew! That does not mean:

1. That he saw you.
2. That he is interested in or attracted to you.

3. That he is available.

4. That opportunity will present.

This conversation may sound ludicrous, but over the years. I've personally seen many women behave this way toward celebrities and other Men At Work. Ladies, if one of these men would respond romantically toward you while at work, and you begin a relationship with one of them, you'd never want them to go to work again. Because you'd expect them to do the same thing again with someone else *while at work*. **Men At Work** are working or should be. If the behavior just discussed brings to you your mind someone who just got out, or maybe on their way to the *nervous hospital* of Billy Bob Thornton fame, don't take it lightly. These are real examples of real things I have seen and see all the time. Women, guard your emotions and fantasies. Don't soul-tie yourself to a wish, a daydream, or an illusion from the imagination of a celebrity promoter.

Women, get real. You really don't have that much confidence in yourself, do you? That's why you choose someone unreachable, untouchable, unattainable that you've never met. And if you were to meet him, it would be in the autograph line. You do this so you can *imagine* having a man--, and a great one at that. In reality, you really don't have one, and you really don't like looking at the fact that you don't.

There are available men in your circle, but so many Lois Lanes don't want Clark Kent, the one they can have. Clark is available; at least you can have a cup of coffee with him, but when he really starts to work when he becomes Superman, that's when you want him.

It's not all about women either. Driving through a nice neighborhood recently, I saw a lawn after lawn being mowed by what appeared to be the woman of the house. I saw trash and tree branches being brought to the curb like so many men, or their things by so many women. The entire neighborhood looked like a women's movie channel. I have renamed it the ***Wifetime Neighborhood.*** Nothing but women. It was a well-off area of town, but there were no men, no Black men. I did see one White man. Yet in that same city, you can travel to see a lower socioeconomic area and see all the Black men in the world. And many of those men appear to be relationships, at least they appear to be with a female in the houses and apartments where they reside. Perhaps those are the men who started or participated in the on-the-job romances and their jobs dead ended. Perhaps they are the men who quit their jobs completely because *Rebecca* had sent some gold bracelets to **him** instead of the other way around. Perhaps they are the men who *retired* after she advertised that she would take care of him. He probably cashed those wolf tickets, and she probably is taking care of him.

Of special concern to me is the man who is doing his job and the woman misconstrues intention. The man who is doing a human services type job where it is his obligation to be kind and caring, can sometimes be at risk. The woman decides that **he** cares for *her* because she's on an ego trip. She then develops a crush, obsession, or soul tie to him. She then may wonder and wander in the Crush-, Obsession-, or Soul Tie-Wilderness for weeks, months, or years.

One such job is that of Pastor. Your married, Pastor is not trying to date you; that's how you know he is a Pastor. If your married, Pastor is He's trying to flirt with you or date you, **he's not a real pastor**. The pastor is the father figure of the church. He does not date or sleep with the children; that's incest. And it does not take a genius to know that *Boyfriend* is not one of the Five-Fold Ministry gifts. Now, if your pastor has to sugarcoat things and *work you* to get you to do work in the church, that's your fault.

If you misread it, that's also your fault. He's not looking for a date any more than my brother Reggie saying, *"You're the sweetest sister I have. Bring me a glass of iced tea."* He's not looking for a date. He's my brother, my relative. Like a pastor who is a relative, spiritually. Of course. my brother could have just asked for the glass of tea, but he's Reggie.

If you don't have discernment yet, get to know the persons with whom you have relationship, so you'll understand how they communicate.

If the people you know don't have appropriate boundaries set, then you set some appropriate ones. If anyone is out of order, you don't also get out of order.

Pastors are at work; they are not at play. They have not come into the House of God on Sunday morning, even though they look good and smell good to look for a date. Just because you came to do nothing and have done nothing for the past 14 years in your church and now that your husband has left you, your new agenda does not mirror the pastor's. Just because the pastor looked your way when he was preaching or touched you on the shoulder when he walked by, those are not romantic overtures. Just because you're coming to church to look for a date doesn't mean that anyone else is, especially the pastor. The pastor's job is to be kind to you. That's his job. He's a Man At Work. If he is sincere, he means well for you. But he's not looking for romantic relationship, especially if he's already married. Don't try to turn God's church into a Wilderness.

I used to be a restaurant server; I went to work. Men who came into the place thought because I and all the other young ladies who worked there were *there*, that we were looking for conversation or invitation. Not the case. I was at work. This is how I learned to respect other people in their jobs and their callings, unfortunately, by being disrespected and mine. I offer people the kind of respect that I want to receive, don't you? Now, especially if you are in your calling, the thing that God has called you to do, you don't take any aspect of your job lightly. You may have fun doing it, but you go to work, to work. No matter where you work or what you do on your job, you go there to work. I never once flirted with or sent signals to a customer to enhance my tip. I only treated them with respect and proficiency. If they misunderstood, that was not on me.

When working as a dentist, are you kidding? A young single woman I was at work. It was the wrong time to bother me with that kind of foolishness. The man who came in after marinating in two or three bottles of cologne--, yes, I asked him to leave. After I started sneezing, he got the picture. It took two days to air my office out.

While taking my office staff to the mall for lunch, we met a man wearing a T-shirt and shorts because he at that very moment worked complacently at the cookie stand. After meeting us and finding out I was single, the only single in the group, he suddenly needed an emergency dental appointment. Another joke--, he went home and put on a three-piece suit and showed up at the office, replete with briefcase, for his urgent appointment. He had perfect teeth and needed a light polish. Some emergency--, Baby, I'm at work--don't bother me!

Another type of Man At Work is the man whom you used to date. Grow up. Just because he was wonderful and patient and kind to you then, and you broke up with him doesn't mean he wants you back. Most of all, realize that the way he treated you was based on *his personality*, not something you brought out in him. If it were because of you, shouldn't you have been able to draw that wonderfulness out of every other guy you've met since then? Get over yourself. If he treated you better than you've ever been treated before, and you left him, wouldn't that make you rather oh--, how shall

I say it in this kind of book? Stupid? There, I said it. Now that he has moved on and is very happy, he is a Man At Work. He is at work and his new relationship, in his new family and his new life. Don't bother a Man At Work.

If you need a reality check, his new wife will help you and you better untie that soul tie before it cuts off your circulation, or air supply.

Women, it's when you behave this way that you give women in general a bad name. That is why a lot of people don't want to claim you. They you embarrass womenfolk, menfolk, kinfolk. It's when you act this way that you get the label that goes with the behavior. Simple, silly, stupid, desperate. It's good that you're driven, but you're driven for social and security reasons. A man is driven about his profession, his career, and his financial status. Those are two different yokes. If you're interfering with his career, finances and opportunity for advancement, you better not be trying to get in his yoke.

And you should not be trying to draw him into *your* yoke. A very worldly man once told me that he's so tired of women throwing themselves at him. He said,

"Sex, who wants it? You can get sex any day of the week, anytime of the day. You can get sex when he can't get bread to eat."

Take a lesson from Rebecca. Let the man ask for you and then send for you when he gets through **working**.

God loves a man at work. How do I know? God was a man at work. For six days and nights He formed, created, and spoke. No woman interrupted Him. No woman tried to intercept Him at the water fountain or in the break room of His job. No woman talked him into taking long lunch or playing hooky in the afternoon to go do something, "fun." No woman bothered God while He was at work. No woman wanted to rock His world-- that He was still in the process of making or had just made.

Check this: ***Wisdom*** was with God from the beginning… **Wisdom is a woman.** She didn't try to "get with God." God was WORKING. Apply Wisdom when you think it's OK to bother a Man At Work; because it's not cool.

Then Jesus came and said that He said and did what He saw the Father do. No woman bothered Jesus, while He was at work--, not with romantic overtures. Yes, women came to Him and worshipped Him as Lord not as a man or a celebrity. True, women came to Him with needs, but because they did not try to trick, distract or date Him, He was able to work, and work out their problems. God loves the man who works.

Women leave the working man to his work.

God At Work

Yet another occasion when a man is at work is when he is being saved, renewed, restored, remade, refreshed, renovated, and rejuvenated by God. While this is happening, leave the man alone while God is working on or with a man. Leave the man alone. Woman, you're risking alienation and being disrespected if you try to interfere when God is working on a man. Like you, men, sometimes require being left alone. When God made man from clay, there was no woman there. Not only was it not necessary for women to be there, men also like that. Men like to be alone, and they *should* like to also be alone with God just as much as you do, maybe more.

When the pot was broken and put back together at the Potter's House, only the man and the one there working on him was the Potter, (Jeremiah 18:4). The only reason the pot could be broken in the first place was that the clay had become hardened from life. So, when a man is going through, when he is at his place of brokenness, know, just like you, he went through a lot to get dry enough, brittle enough, and fragile enough to break.

And after being broken, when he is being put back together, when God is working on him, woman, I say this in love, **Step aside**.

The application: Women stay out of Men's Conferences and seminars. Wives do not hinder him from going. Do not lay a guilt trip and do not go into the auditorium and sit in the back. God has much work to do on His men. And your presence is a spectator may inhibit them, and the process. Your presence is not helping the man of God. Get out of the way. He doesn't need a mother. His mother is probably what caused 100% of his problem in the first place. Remember if he's

Wilderness he may already have a 300% problem. Don't make it into a 400% problem by getting in there too.

Women. Even if you're married to the biggest Wilderness Man of all time, even if he's the most **Wildernessy** of all Wildernesses, go home and spend time in the presence of God letting God work on you. You married him. If your mate is that bad, find out why you married him and what's wrong with you. Get it straight who is supposed to be the object of your first romantic desire.

After Salvation, when the Holy Spirit is at work on your man or any man, don't bother Him or him. Quench not the Holy Spirit of God. If you're in a family service and your husband falls out under the anointing, don't come up and rub his head. Hands off! That's very distracting. Leave the man alone. When he's ready for you, he'll call you, come get you, or send for you. If you behave as a Rebecca, maybe there's a bracelet or some nice jewelry in it for you.

While he's at work if you don't respect the man, he will not respect you. And you're likely to call forth a lot of trouble to yourself by those whom God put in place to make sure no one disturbs His Man At Work.

You don't want a half-made man any more than you want a half-baked cake. Also, a male who's a Man-by-Faith. Leave him alone and let faith have its perfect work.

Other books by this author:

AK: The Adventures of the Agape Kid

AMONG SOME THIEVES

Churchzilla, *the Wanna-Be, Supposed-to-be Bride of Christ*

Demons Hate Questions

Don't Refuse Me, Lord (4 book series)

Don't Say That to Me

every apple

The Fold (4 book series)

> **The Fold (Book 1)**
>
> **Name Your Seed (Book 2)**
>
> **The Poor Attitudes of Money (Book 4)**
>
> **Do Not Orphan Your Seed**

got HEALING?

got LOVE?

got money?

How to Dental Assist

Let Me Have A Dollar's Worth

Man Safari, *The*

Marriage Ed. *Rules of Engagement & Marriage*

Made Perfect in Love

Power Money: Nine Times the Tithe

The Power of Wealth *(forthcoming)*

Seasons of Grief

Seasons of War *(forthcoming)*

The Spirit of Poverty *(forthcoming)*

Warfare Prayer Against Poverty

When the Devourer is Rebuked

The Wilderness Romance *(3-book series)*

    The Social Wilderness

    The Sexual Wilderness

    The Spiritual Wilderness

Journals & Devotionals by this author:

The Cool of the Day – *Journal for times spent with God*

He Hears Us, Prayer Journal *in 4 different colors*

I Have A Star, Dream Journal *kids, teen, young adult & up.*

I Have A Star, Guided Prayer Journal, *2 styles: Boy or Girl*

J'ai une Etoile, Journal des Reves

Let Her Dream, Dream Journal *in multiple cover colors*

Men Shall Dream, Dream Journal, *(blue or black)*

My Favorite Prayers (multiple covers)

My Sowing Journal (in three different colors)

Tengo una Estrella, Diario de Sueños

Wise Counsel (Journal in 2 styles)

<u>Illustrated children's books by this author:</u>

Be the Lion (3-book series)

Big Dog (8-book series)

Do Not Say That to Me

Every Apple

Fluff the Clouds

I Love You All Over the World

Imma Dance

The Jump Rope

Kiss the Sun

The Masked Man

Not During a Pandemic

Push the Wind

Slide

Tangled Taffy

What If?

Wiggle, Wiggle; Giggle, Giggle

Worry About Yourself

You Did Not Say Goodbye to Me

Notes

www.ingramcontent.com/pod-product-compliance
Lightning Source LLC
Chambersburg PA
CBHW050352280326
41933CB00010BA/1435